Sunny-Side Up!
Uplifting Christian Essays
Charles E. Cravey

In His Steps Publishing Company

Copyright © 2025 by Charles Edward Cravey.

All rights reserved.

No portion of this book may be reproduced in any form without written permission from the publisher or author, except as permitted by U.S. copyright law.

All scripture is from the King James Version of the Holy Bible unless otherwise noted.

ISBN: 978-1-58535-094-0 (Paperback

ISBN: 978-1-58535-095-7 (Kindle)

Library of Congress Catalog Number: 2025915152

Printed in the United States of America

Published by In His Steps Publishing, Statesboro, Georgia.

Contents

Dedication	V
Preface	VII
1. Finding Light in Dark Times	1
2. Joyful Gratitude	10
3. The Beauty of Grace	18
4. Hope and Healing	25
5. Purposeful Living	32
6. Community and Connection	39
7. Forgiveness	46
8. Faith and Fear	53
9. The Blessing of Trials	60
10. Sharing Your light	66
11. Biblical Joy	73
12. Trusting God's Timing	81
13. Worship in Everyday Life	88
14. Living in Hope	95

15. Spreading Sunshine	102
Afterword	111

Dedication

To my neighbors and friends, whose front porches have become classrooms of grace.

To my family, whose open doors and open hearts model the love of Christ.

To every soul who pauses for a shared cup of sweet tea—may this book carry that same welcome into your home and heart.

Preface

From the front porch of my childhood home, I learned that faith often blooms in the space between neighbors' hellos and the hush of late afternoon. It taught me that holy moments are woven into everyday rhythms, like a breeze stirring the jasmine vines overhead. Front-porch faith is not a solo pursuit but a warm circle of shared lives and whispered prayers.

Within these pages, you will find fifteen chapters that journey through darkness, gratitude, grace, healing, purpose, community, forgiveness, faith, trials, light-sharing, joy, timing, worship, hope, and kindness.

Each chapter pairs a reflective sonnet, a grounding Scripture, and a heartfelt closing prayer, designed to stir your imagination, root your soul in Scripture, and guide your conversations with God. Whether read aloud in solitude or shared with friends over fresh-squeezed lemonade, these words are meant to become the gentle cadence of your daily walk.

Use this book like a comfortable bench under an old oak—come and rest, linger, and be refreshed. Allow the poetry to linger on your lips in the morning calm, lean into the prayer when dusk settles in your heart, and let the Scripture echo in your mind as you serve those around you. There is no set speed to this journey; move at your own pace, return often, and sit where the light feels brightest.

My prayer is that this book becomes a trusted companion, a friend who pauses at your side to remind you of God's steadfast love. May it inspire you to open your door more freely, offer grace more generously, and embrace the simple joys that surround you. May these pages draw you into deeper communion with the God who meets us best on the front porch of our own hearts.

1
Finding Light in Dark Times

The Power of Faith

"The Lord is close to the brokenhearted and saves those who are crushed in spirit."

—Psalm 34:18

In the tapestry of human experience, dark times often serve as the backdrop against which the human spirit shines its brightest.

Historical events, personal struggles, and the collective challenges faced by communities expose the fragility of hope, yet within these moments of despair, many find the profound and transformative power of faith. Faith, often defined as a strong belief in something, transcends religious boundaries and resonates deeply within the individual psyche, providing not just solace but also a pathway to resilience.

The Nature of Dark Times

Dark times are inevitable in life; they manifest as periods of loss, grief, confusion, or societal upheaval. The global pandemic, political turmoil, economic crises, and personal tragedies act as catalysts for emotional turmoil and moral questioning.

These experiences can leave individuals feeling isolated and hopeless, often prompting existential inquiries about meaning and purpose. In such moments, the act of turning to faith can serve as a beacon of light, illuminating paths that may have seemed obscured by darkness.

The Role of Faith

Faith operates on multiple levels. It can be religious, spiritual, or simply a steadfast belief in the goodness of humanity and the potential for positive change. Throughout history, faith has galvanized communities, providing a shared sense of identity and purpose.

For example, during the civil rights movement in the United States, leaders such as Martin Luther King Jr. drew upon their religious faith to inspire peaceful resistance against systemic oppression. His belief in justice rooted in a higher moral ground motivated countless individuals to join the fight for equality, highlighting how faith can mobilize collective action in dark times.

On a personal level, faith can offer comfort and hope. Individuals who face terminal illness, the loss of loved ones, or severe personal crises often turn to faith as a source of strength. This is poignantly illustrated in the stories of those who have undergone remarkable personal transformations after hitting rock bottom.

Many recount how their faith—whether in a religious figure, the universe, or the inherent goodness of life—provided them with the courage to continue, to seek healing, and to find new purpose. These narratives underscore the notion that faith, while deeply personal, can also ripple outward, fostering connections and community.

Psychological and Emotional Benefits

The psychological benefits of faith during tumultuous times are well-documented. Faith can act as a buffer against stress, providing individuals with a sense of control in unpredictable circumstances.

Research shows that those who engage in faith-based practices such as prayer, meditation, or community worship often experience lower levels of anxiety and depression. This psychological resilience stems from the belief that there is a greater plan or purpose behind suffering, which can transform the narrative from one of despair to one of hope.

Moreover, faith encourages a mindset of gratitude and acceptance, key components in navigating life's challenges. By recognizing that adversity can lead to growth, individuals cultivate a perspective that allows them to find meaning in suffering. This shift can lead to personal development and a strengthened sense of identity, as people leverage their experiences to foster empathy and compassion for others in similar situations.

The Modern Context

In contemporary society, where uncertainty often reigns, the search for faith—whether religious or secular—is increasingly relevant. Many seek communities that provide a sense of belonging and shared belief, especially during times of crisis.

Social media has enabled the proliferation of faith-based support networks, where individuals can share their stories, seek guidance, and uplift one another. These online spaces often create a sense of collective faith that transcends geographical barriers, highlighting the power of community in fostering resilience and hope.

Yet, it is crucial to acknowledge that not everyone finds comfort in traditional notions of faith. Some individuals may find solace in philosophy, science, or human connection.

The essence of finding light in dark times lies in the universality of resilience—the understanding that regardless of the source of faith, the pursuit of hope and meaning is a fundamental aspect of the human condition.

Conclusion

Faith acts as a powerful tool for navigating dark times, transforming despair into resilience, and fostering hope amidst adversity.

Whether derived from religious beliefs, personal philosophies, or the strength of community, faith encourages individuals to transcend their circumstances and find light—even in the darkest of moments.

As we continue to face challenges in our lives and societies, embracing the diverse forms of faith can serve as a reminder of our shared humanity and our innate capacity for hope and renewal. In the words of poet Maya Angelou, "I can be changed by what happens to me. But I refuse to be reduced by it." In this refusal lies the true power of faith.

Light in the Shadows

Charles E. Cravey

When twilight dims the path our hearts must tread,
And shadows gather deep within the soul,
Faith whispers soft where earthly hopes have fled,
A steady flame that makes the broken whole.

The weary cry, "Where shall my refuge be?"
Yet grace arrives on wings not seen but known,
A balm to heal, a bond to set us free,
Through trials faced, we find we're not alone.

The stars above once pierced the stormy night.
As humble shepherds watched with holy gaze.
So too may we behold redeeming light,
When lifted up by mercy's quiet blaze.

In darkest hours, God's love will still abide —
A constant guide where fear and doubt divide.

Closing Prayer: A Light That Leads

Gracious Lord,
As we journey through life's valleys, may we remember that Your light is never extinguished by darkness. In sorrow, give us peace; in trials, grant us courage; and in confusion, restore our hope. Let this chapter be a testament to Your sustaining power—that when the night feels long, Your presence dawns anew with every breath.

Help us walk boldly in faith, uplifting those beside us, and embracing the path You've set before us. May readers feel Your comfort and discover that even in silence and stillness, Your voice speaks clearly. Let the stories shared here be seeds of strength, planted in the soil of grace.

In Your holy name we pray, Amen.

2
Joyful Gratitude

Cultivating a Heart of Thankfulness

"Give thanks in all circumstances; for this is God's will for you in Christ Jesus."

— 1 Thessalonians 5:18

In a world that often seems dominated by chaos and negativity, the practice of gratitude stands as a beacon of hope and positivity. To cultivate a heart of thankfulness is to embrace a joyful perspective on life, one that recognizes and appreciates the myriad blessings we often take for granted. Joyful gratitude is not merely an emotional response; it is an intentional practice that can have transformative effects on our well-being, relationships, and overall outlook on life.

Understanding Gratitude

At its core, gratitude is the recognition of the goodness in our lives. This goodness can manifest in various forms, from the kindness of friends and family to the beauty of nature and the simple pleasures of everyday life. Psychologists have long studied gratitude and found that expressing it can lead to increased happiness and reduced stress. Gratitude shifts our focus from what is lacking in our lives to what is abundant, creating a positive feedback loop that bolsters our mental health.

Every gratitude practice begins with reflection. Take a moment each day to contemplate what you are thankful for. Whether big or small, acknowledging these points of gratitude can help to foster a mindset that appreciates the present moment. This shift in perspective is crucial; by focusing on what we have rather than what we lack, we nurture a sense of contentment and joy.

The Science of Gratitude

Research has consistently shown that gratitude is linked to numerous mental and physical health benefits. A study by Emmons and McCullough (2003) demonstrated that individuals who regularly practiced gratitude reported feeling more optimistic, experiencing fewer symptoms of depression, and engaging in more pro-social behaviors. Furthermore, gratitude can enhance relationships; showing appreciation to those around us can strengthen bonds and foster a supportive social network.

The physiological effects are just as compelling. Gratitude has been associated with better sleep, improved immune function, and decreased feelings of anxiety and depression. When we express gratitude, our brain releases neurotransmitters like dopamine and serotonin, which are known to enhance mood and overall emotional well-being.

Cultivating a Heart of Thankfulness

To cultivate a heart of thankfulness, one must integrate gratitude into daily life. Here are some practical strategies:

1. **Gratitude Journaling:** Dedicate a few minutes each day to write down things you are grateful for. This practice can serve as a positive reminder during challenging times.

2. **Mindfulness and Meditation:** Engage in mindfulness practices that promote an awareness of the present moment. Meditation focused on gratitude allows individuals to reflect on their blessings deeply.

3. **Express Appreciation:** Don't just feel grateful; express it. Tell your loved ones what you appreciate about them. This not only strengthens relationships but also reinforces your gratitude pathways.

4. **Social Media Acknowledgements:** In a digital age, expressing gratitude through social media can have widespread effects.

Sharing moments of thankfulness publicly encourages others to do the same, creating a community of gratefulness.

5. **Acts of Kindness:** Engage in acts of kindness towards others. When you give back, you reinforce the cycle of gratitude. Helping others can boost your own sense of happiness and fulfillment.

The Ripple Effect of Gratitude

Gratitude has a profound ripple effect. When we cultivate thankfulness, it not only impacts our individual lives but can also influence those around us. A culture of gratitude can transform communities, fostering environments of support and positivity. In workplaces, for instance, grateful individuals are found to be more productive, collaborative, and committed.

In families, a focus on appreciation can nurture deeper connections and enhance emotional resilience. By instilling a gratitude practice in children from a young age, we can guide the next generation toward a mindset that values kindness, empathy, and connection.

Conclusion

In conclusion, joyful gratitude is a powerful practice that enriches our lives and the lives of those around us. By consciously cultivating a heart of thankfulness, we unlock the potential for greater happiness, improved mental and physical health, and stronger relationships.

As we navigate life's challenges and triumphs, let us remember to pause and reflect on the abundance that surrounds us—a gift that, when acknowledged, transforms our experience of the world from mere existence to one filled with joy and appreciation. Through the practice of gratitude, we create a life that is not only happier but also richer and more meaningful.

The Garden of Thanks

Charles E. Cravey

Where morning light paints gold on leaf and vine,
And silence hums a song of grateful grace,
The heart awakened sees each breath as sign—
A gift divine in ordinary space.

The sparrow's flight, the laughter shared in rain,
The kindness born from love's enduring flame,
These moments bloom through joy and not through gain.
As praise and peace grow rooted in God's name.

No riches match the wealth of thankful hearts,
Whose gaze lifts high beyond the fleeting dust.
In gratitude, the miracle imparts
A hope secure—a promise we can trust.

So let each step be watered with delight,
And gratitude make every burden light.

Closing Prayer: A Heart That Rejoices

Heavenly Father,

Thank You for the beauty hidden in each day, the quiet blessings that often pass unseen, and the joy that flourishes when we pause to reflect. Teach us to nurture grateful hearts—not only in moments of celebration, but also through seasons of challenge. Help us to recognize Your presence in the simple and the sacred, the whispered kindness and the unspoken grace.

May this chapter call our readers to live with open hands, receiving and giving Your goodness freely. Let our gratitude become a testimony—a light shining in homes, churches, and communities. Shape us into people who choose joy, not because life is easy, but because Your love makes us strong. In Jesus' name we pray, Amen.

3
The Beauty of Grace

Embracing God's Unconditional Love

"But he said to me, 'My grace is sufficient for you, for my power is made perfect in weakness.'" — 2 Corinthians 12:9

In a world often marked by conditions and limitations, the concept of grace emerges as a radiant beacon of hope and transformation. Grace, at its core, signifies unmerited favor, a gift freely bestowed upon humanity by God. It transcends the barriers that we, as individuals, impose upon one another and ourselves, reflecting an all-encompassing love that invites us to embrace our spiritual identity and find solace in our imperfections.

Understanding and embracing God's unconditional love through the lens of grace can profoundly affect our lives and those around us.

The idea of grace is woven intricately into the fabric of various religious paradigms, yet its essence remains universally relatable. In Christianity, for example, grace is a central theme that manifests most strikingly in the teachings and actions of Jesus Christ.

Through His sacrifice, believers are offered redemption and forgiveness, not based on their actions or worthiness, but rooted in God's innate love for humanity. This unconditional love challenges our societal inclination to earn affection through deeds and accomplishments, reminding us that we are valuable not for what we do, but for who we are.

Embracing grace requires a shift in perspective. It beckons us to relinquish the burdens of self-judgment and performance-driven validation. The beauty of grace lies in its invitation to surrender our flawed humanity to a divine affection that sees beyond our mistakes. In this process, we can find liberation from the shackles of guilt and shame, allowing us to cultivate a deeper understanding of ourselves and foster compassion towards others. This transformation often manifests through acts of kindness, as those who genuinely grasp the depth of grace are more inclined to extend it to their fellow beings.

Moreover, grace teaches us the value of humility. Recognizing that we are recipients of such profound love instills a sense of gratitude that can change the narrative of our lives. When we accept grace, we are reminded that vulnerability does not diminish our worth; instead, it enhances our authenticity.

This acceptance allows us to reach out to others, to empathize with their struggles, and to offer support born from our own experiences of receiving grace. Such connections build a sense of community, reinforcing the idea that we are all on a shared journey marked by trials, tribulations, and ultimately, the relentless pursuit of love.

In a practical sense, the recognition of grace in our lives can manifest through daily actions that embody love and acceptance. It might appear as a comforting presence extended to someone in distress or the forgiveness offered to a friend who has erred. These gestures, however small, ripple through the fabric of our communities, creating a culture that prizes understanding over judgment and reconciliation over bitterness.

When we nurture grace, we cultivate an environment where individuals feel seen, valued, and cherished—regardless of their past or current circumstances.

The beauty of grace is that it is both a gift and a call to action. As we experience this divine love, we are prompted to reflect it in our relationships and interactions. This cyclical nature of grace—receiving and giving—creates an enduring legacy of compassion that can transcend generations.

When we embrace God's unconditional love, we participate in a divine dance that invites all of humanity to join, celebrating our differences while recognizing our shared essence as beings deserving of love.

In conclusion, grace is not merely a theological concept; it is a transformative power that invites us to live lives unmarred by guilt and shame and filled with love and acceptance. By embracing grace, we encounter the beauty of God's unconditional love, which has the potential to heal, unite, and inspire.

This journey towards understanding grace is a lifelong endeavor, but the rewards—inner peace, authentic relationships, and a loving community—make the pursuit worthwhile. In a world that often propagates division, let us be ambassadors of grace, opening our hearts to the beauty of unconditional love and extending that love to all.

The Unfolding of Grace

Charles E. Cravey

When weary hearts are burdened by regret,
And silent shame has rooted in the soul,
Grace enters in—a love we can't forget,
That sweeps the dust and gently makes us whole.

Not earned by deed nor measured by our worth,
It flows like rain on soil parched by pain.
Unbidden, yet it brings a second birth,
Restoring hope where loss and guilt have lain.

So let us kneel before this wondrous tide,
Not with proud claim, but humble, open hands.
For grace, once tasted, never will divide—
It draws all near and lovingly expands.

In grace we find the truest kind of peace.
And through its light, our heavy sorrows cease.

Closing Prayer: A Heart Surrendered to Grace

Lord of Unfailing Love,

We thank You for the grace that finds us in our weakest moments and lifts us beyond what we could never earn. Teach us to surrender—not in defeat, but in holy trust. Remove the weight of perfectionism and performance and draw us near with Your quiet compassion.

Let this chapter inspire hearts to rest in Your mercy and reflect that love to others. May grace become not just something we receive, but something we live: forgiving, understanding, and embracing with joy. Help us release our fears and walk boldly in the light of Your unconditional love. In Jesus' name we pray, Amen.

4
Hope and Healing

Stories of Redemption

"He heals the brokenhearted and binds up their wounds."
— **Psalm 147:3**

Throughout human history, the themes of hope and healing have played a pivotal role in shaping narratives that resonate with our deepest emotions. Stories of redemption remind us that regardless of our past mistakes or struggles, the possibility of renewal and transformation is always within reach.

This essay explores the fundamental aspects of hope and healing through compelling stories that illustrate how individuals can emerge victorious from their darkest moments.

The Power of Personal Narrative

One of the most profound ways we experience hope and healing is through personal narratives. Every individual carries a unique story, often laden with challenges and setbacks. Take the story of John, a young man who battled addiction for a decade. The depths of his despair left him isolated from family and friends, entrenched in a cycle of destructive behavior.

Yet, it was during a moment of vulnerability, surrounded by the remnants of his past, that John found a flicker of hope. He enrolled in a rehabilitation program, where he not only confronted his demons but also discovered a community of individuals eager to support one another.

His journey illustrates how recognizing one's struggles and seeking help can illuminate a path toward redemption. John's story is a testament to the resilience of the human spirit, as he transitioned from a life of despair to one where healing became his mantra.

Collective Healing Through Community

While personal journeys of redemption are powerful, they are often amplified within a communal context. The impact of sharing stories of hope among groups can foster collective healing. Consider the narrative of a support group for survivors of trauma. Each participant carries their own burdens, yet as they gather each week, the stories exchanged serve as catalysts for healing. In this safe space, vulnerability is met with compassion, and empathy fuels resilience.

The stories of these survivors highlight the importance of community in the healing process; as they listen to one another, they realize they are not alone in their suffering. This collective aspect of redemption highlights how hope can be nurtured in the presence of others, paving the way for healing.

The Role of Forgiveness

Another critical component of redemption is forgiveness. Holding onto anger and resentment can be burdensome and impede our ability to heal. The story of Maria, who faced betrayal by a close friend, exemplifies this point. Initially, Maria was consumed by feelings of hurt and betrayal, allowing these emotions to define her.

However, through reflection and a desire for inner peace, she chose to forgive her friend. This act of forgiveness did not condone the betrayal but freed Maria from the shackles of her pain. Her experience illustrates that forgiveness is not solely for those who have wronged us; it is a gift we give ourselves, allowing space for hope and renewal in our hearts.

The Journey of Self-Discovery

Redemption often intertwines with self-discovery. Many individuals find that their struggles become the catalyst for profound personal growth. For instance, consider the story of Ahmed, who, after losing his job, experienced a significant identity crisis. Initially devastated, he embarked on a journey to rediscover his passions and purpose. Through this exploration, Ahmed found solace in helping others who faced similar hardships; he volunteered at local shelters and started a blog sharing his experiences.

In helping others, Ahmed not only healed himself but also inspired hope in those around him. His transformation underscores the idea that through adversity, we can unearth our true potential and contribute positively to the world.

Conclusion

Hope and healing are integral to the human experience, beautifully illustrated through stories of redemption. Whether through personal struggles, communal support, acts of forgiveness, or journeys of self-discovery, these narratives remind us that the road to healing is paved with resilience and courage.

Each story serves as a beacon of hope, encouraging others to embrace their own paths to redemption. The power of hope lies in its ability to illuminate the darkest corners of our lives, guiding us toward healing and a renewed sense of purpose. In celebrating these stories, we acknowledge the strength of the human spirit and the enduring possibility of transformation.

From Ashes to Morning

Charles E. Cravey

When night of sorrow shrouds the weary soul,
And yearning hearts feel lost in empty gloom,
Hope stirs within as broken pieces whole.
A gentle light that banishes the tomb.

Through tales of grace redeemed, our spirits rise,
Like seeds reborn in earth once dry and bare,

Each story weaves a song of sacrifice,
And paints new colors on the canvas there.

The wounds we bear find balm in mercy's stream.
In loving hands that bind with tender care,
Where faith alights upon a healing dream,
And broken hearts find strength where promise stands.

So let this truth resound both near and far:
In every scar, God's glory is a star.

Closing Prayer: A Prayer of Redeeming Hope

Heavenly Father of Compassion,
We stand before You weighed by wounds unseen.
In Your embrace our fractured hopes find rest,
Your love revives the heart and mends the seam.

Teach us to bear one another's burdens softly.
To bring Your healing touch with tender care.
May every story of redemption guide us on.
And every healed heart praises Your presence there.

In Jesus' name we pray, Amen.

5
Purposeful Living

Discovering God's Plan for You

"For we are God's handiwork, created in Christ Jesus to do good works, which God prepared in advance for us to do."
— **Ephesians 2:10**

In a world often characterized by chaos and uncertainty, many individuals find themselves yearning for a sense of purpose. Questions about one's existence and the greater meaning of life can lead to profound introspection. As we navigate our daily routines and face the trials of life, the pursuit of discovering God's plan for us can serve as a guiding light, illuminating our path and helping us fulfill our potential.

At the core of purposeful living lies the belief that our lives have significant meaning, shaped by divine intention. Understanding God's plan is a journey that involves self-reflection, prayer, and engagement with sacred texts. It encourages us to look beyond our immediate circumstances and recognize the larger tapestry of life woven by God's hand. Through introspective practices, we can begin to uncover our unique gifts and talents, which play a vital role in the divine narrative.

One essential aspect of discovering God's plan is understanding our inherent value. Each individual is created with purpose; recognizing this can empower us to embrace our identities fully. Scriptures remind us that we are fearfully and wonderfully made (Psalm 139:14), instilling a sense of worth and responsibility.

This realization encourages us to cultivate our talents and pursue objectives that align with both our passions and the values we hold dear. When we acknowledge our gifts, we open ourselves to opportunities where we can serve others, reflecting God's love and purpose through our actions.

Additionally, the journey of discovering God's plan is often enriched by community. Surrounding ourselves with like-minded individuals who share our faith can provide support and encouragement as we seek clarity in our lives.

Engaging in fellowship fosters accountability and nurtures a collective pursuit of divine purpose. Churches and spiritual organizations often provide resources, guidance, and mentorship, becoming fertile ground for growth and exploration. These communal bonds remind us that we are not alone in our quest; rather, we are part of a larger family united by faith.

Another critical component of purposeful living is the willingness to listen and be guided by God. This necessitates a posture of humility and openness, allowing divine wisdom to direct our choices. Prayer serves as the communication channel through which we can express our desires, concerns, and dreams, seeking alignment with God's vision rather than our limited understanding.

As we cultivate a consistent prayer life, we become more attuned to the subtle nudges and signs that signal God's direction, helping us to navigate the complexities of life with greater faith and assurance.

Moreover, the practice of gratitude can illuminate our understanding of God's plan. By recognizing and appreciating the gifts we have received, even in moments of struggle, we can develop a perspective that appreciates the journey as much as the destination.

Gratitude shifts our focus from what we lack to the abundance present in our lives, fostering a sense of contentment. This mindset transforms our challenges into opportunities for spiritual growth and deeper insight into God's overarching plan.

Lastly, embracing the concept of service can profoundly impact our pursuit of purposeful living. We are called to be stewards of God's creation, using our talents to serve others and advance the greater good. Acts of kindness, compassion, and generosity create ripples of change in our communities and beyond, fulfilling the command to love one another (John 13:34). As we extend ourselves in service, we engage in a mission that transcends personal fulfillment, aligning ourselves with the heart of God's plan to reach and transform the world around us.

In conclusion, discovering God's plan for our lives is a multi-faceted journey involving self-awareness, community support, prayer, gratitude, and service. As we embrace these elements, we can develop a deeper understanding of our purpose and fulfill our roles in the divine narrative.

Purposeful living not only enriches our lives but also enables us to contribute positively to the lives of others, reflecting the love and purpose that God instills in each of us. Ultimately, it is through this journey that we can live lives imbued with meaning, joy, and fulfillment, walking confidently in the destiny designed for us.

The Weaver's Design

Charles E. Cravey

When dawn unveils the tapestry of days,
With threads of purpose in each subtle hue,
Our Maker's hands inscribe on hearts His ways,
And weave a path unique for me and you.

Though storms may fray the edges of our dreams,
His steady fingers mend with patient art.
Each trial refines the gold of what He deems,
Aligning clay to form His perfect heart.

No shadow stands outside His watchful gaze,
Nor loss escapes the wisdom of His plan.
In every step, His love directs our days.
Entrusting gifts that bloom at His command.

So, walk in faith, adorned by heaven's light,
Each life a stitch within His grand design.

Closing Prayer: A Journey Aligned with His Will

Heavenly Weaver of All,
Thank You for the purpose You embed in every soul. Guide our hearts to seek Your will with humble trust. Open our eyes to recognize the gifts and passions You have bestowed.

Let us serve with joy, love without reserve, and follow faithfully along the path You have ordained. Grant us courage when uncertainty calls, wisdom when we face choices, and contentment in walking daily by Your hand. In Jesus' name we pray, Amen.

6
Community and Connection

The Strength of Fellowship

"And let us consider how to stir up one another to love and good works, not neglecting to meet together." — **Hebrews 10:24-25**

In an increasingly digital world, where social media often masquerades as genuine interaction, the essential values of community and connection have emerged as pillars for a fulfilling and resilient life. These values, embodied in the concept of fellowship, not only enrich our individual experiences but also lay the groundwork for a more harmonious society.

This essay explores the profound impact of community and connection, illustrating how fellowship strengthens our bonds, fosters personal growth, and cultivates resilience in the face of adversity.

At the heart of every community lies a shared sense of belonging—a feeling that one is part of something greater than themselves. This sense of belonging is often cultivated through fellowship, where individuals come together around common interests, beliefs, or goals.

Whether it is through local organizations, clubs, religious institutions, or volunteer groups, fellowship fosters connections that transcend individual differences. As highlighted by sociologist Robert Putnam in his book "Bowling Alone," the decline in community engagement over the last few decades has contributed to a decrease in social trust and connectedness, leading to isolation and loneliness.

Conversely, thriving communities, characterized by active fellowship, exhibit enhanced social cohesion and support, leading to improved mental and emotional well-being for their members.

Moreover, fellowship plays a critical role in personal growth and development. When individuals engage with their communities, they are often challenged to step outside their comfort zones and embrace new perspectives. This interaction fosters empathy and understanding, allowing people to learn from each other's experiences.

For example, community service initiatives not only meet the needs of those less fortunate but also provide participants with profound insights into the struggles and triumphs of their neighbors. Such experiences can be transformative, leading individuals to become better versions of themselves. In this context, fellowship becomes a powerful force for personal and collective evolution, proving that through connection, we can grow and thrive.

In times of crisis, the strength of fellowship becomes even more apparent. Historical events have shown us that communities rally together in the face of adversity, demonstrating resilience and solidarity. For instance, during natural disasters, communities that foster strong connections often respond more effectively by providing mutual aid, emotional support, and resources to those in need.

The COVID-19 pandemic starkly revealed the importance of community and connection. As people found themselves physically isolated, many turned to virtual platforms to maintain fellowship, demonstrating the unyielding human desire for connection. Initiatives such as neighborhood support groups and online social gatherings emerged, highlighting how adaptable community bonds can be even in the most challenging circumstances. Such resilience is a testament to the power of connection—when individuals unite, they can overcome even the most daunting challenges.

Furthermore, fostering a spirit of fellowship contributes to the collective well-being of society. Communities that prioritize cooperation and mutual respect tend to be more inclusive and equitable. As individuals learn to appreciate diverse perspectives, they cultivate a culture of acceptance and understanding, reducing social tensions and conflicts.

Educational programs that emphasize teamwork and community engagement, such as those found in schools and universities, play a pivotal role in shaping the values of future generations. By instilling the importance of fellowship early on, we can create a society that values interconnectedness and stands united against divisive ideologies.

In conclusion, the strength of community and connection lies in the spirit of fellowship. As we navigate an ever-changing world, it is crucial to prioritize these values, recognizing their profound impact on our individual lives and collective society. Through belonging, personal growth, resilience in adversity, and the promotion of inclusivity, fellowship fosters a deeper understanding of our shared humanity.

By nurturing these connections, we can build a more compassionate and cohesive world, where each individual feels valued and empowered, contributing to the strength of the communities around them. Thus, let us embrace the power of community and fellowship as we work towards a brighter future, one connection at a time.

The Strength of Fellowship

Charles E. Cravey

When weary souls find comfort in the fold,
And hearts once lone unite in trust and care,
A tapestry of faith and hope untold,
Woven by hands that seek and strive to share.

Each kindly word, a thread of gold so fine,
Each open door, a beacon shining bright.
Together through the storms, our souls entwine,
And in our bonds, we find our God's delight.

No barrier of pain or fear can hold,
When love sustains the fellowship we bear;

> For as one body, in one heart enrolled,
> We rise above despair in earnest prayer.
>
> So let us walk as friends in grace and truth,
> Renewed in strength by unity's sweet proof.

Closing Prayer: A Prayer for Unified Hearts

Heavenly Father of Unity and Love,
We thank You for the gift of community and the bonds that lift our spirits. Teach us to honor one another, bearing burdens with compassion and celebrating joys with gratitude. Let our fellowship reflect Your heart, drawing us closer to You and to each other.

Guide us to serve with humble hands and open hearts, that our gatherings become sanctuaries of grace. May every act of kindness and every shared meal testify to Your presence among us, strengthening the body of Christ in unity and purpose. In Jesus' name we pray, Amen.

7
Forgiveness

The Pathway to Freedom

"Be kind and compassionate to one another, forgiving each other, just as in Christ God forgave you." — **Ephesians 4:32**

Forgiveness is a powerful act, often viewed as a gift we extend to others. However, it is even more profound in its role as a liberating force within us. In a world rife with conflict, grudges, and emotional burdens, the act of forgiving can serve as a pathway to freedom—a means of releasing the chains of resentment and anger that bind us. This essay explores the complexities of forgiveness, its psychological benefits, and how it can lead to a more peaceful and fulfilling life.

At its core, forgiveness is about letting go. When we hold onto grudges, we allow our past experiences, often painful and traumatic, to dictate our present and future. These lingering feelings can manifest in several ways: through stress, anxiety, and a general sense of unhappiness.

The weight of unresolved grievances can feel like a heavy burden, inhibiting our ability to fully engage with life. By forgiving those who have wronged us, we release ourselves from this burden, allowing for emotional healing and personal growth.

From a psychological perspective, research has shown that forgiveness can lead to significant mental health benefits. Studies indicate that individuals who practice forgiveness are less likely to experience depression and anxiety. They often report higher levels of self-esteem and overall life satisfaction.

This is largely because forgiveness promotes a mindset of compassion and understanding, fostering healthier relationships with others and, most importantly, with oneself. When we forgive, we shift our focus from victimhood to agency, reclaiming our power to choose how we respond to our circumstances.

Forgiveness is not synonymous with condoning wrongdoing or excusing the behavior of others. It does not mean forgetting the harm done or reconciling with those who violated our trust. Instead, it is an inward journey of understanding and acceptance. It requires us to confront our feelings and acknowledge our pain while also recognizing that holding onto resentment serves no constructive purpose.

Embracing forgiveness involves a conscious decision to prioritize our own emotional well-being over the desire for retribution or justice.

Moreover, the act of forgiving can be deeply transformative. It invites us to cultivate empathy and compassion, not only for others but also for ourselves. This is particularly important in a society that often encourages a culture of blame and dissatisfaction.

When we choose to forgive, we model resilience and encourage a more understanding and humane approach to conflict and relationships. Such a shift can create a ripple effect, inspiring others to embrace forgiveness, thereby fostering a more supportive and compassionate community.

In many cultures and philosophies, forgiveness is viewed as a spiritual practice that can lead to enlightenment and liberation. Various religious traditions emphasize the importance of forgiveness as a means to attain inner peace and connection with the divine.

This spiritual dimension of forgiveness highlights its role in transcending the ego and moving towards a state of love and unity. By releasing our grievances, we align ourselves with a higher purpose and contribute to a more harmonious existence.

In conclusion, forgiveness is indeed a pathway to freedom. It frees us from the emotional shackles of resentment, empowering us to live fully and authentically. By embracing forgiveness, we unlock the potential for profound healing, both individually and collectively.

As we navigate the complexities of human relationships, let us remember that in choosing to forgive, we choose to free ourselves, allowing love and understanding to guide our lives. In this way, forgiveness becomes not just an act of kindness towards others, but a vital key to our own liberation and happiness.

The Pathway to Freedom

Charles E. Cravey

When chains of anger bind the heavy heart,
And memories of pain convulse the soul,
Forgiveness breaks the lock and bids depart
The weight of grief, restoring hope made whole.

To grant release, to let the past unwind,
This humble gift becomes a healing balm.
No bitter root can choke a softened mind,
Nor bruise endure where mercy brings its calm.

As dawn dispels the shadows of the night,
So, pardon scatters darkness from the mind.
Through grace we walk within undying light,
And in forgiving, truest peace we find.

So let us give the gift that sets us free—
Forgiveness blooms, a flower of mercy.

Closing Prayer: A Prayer of Mercy and Release

Heavenly Father of Infinite Compassion,
We come before You with hearts weighed by hurt and longing for relief.
Teach us to lay our burdens at Your feet and to extend the same grace You've lavished on us.
Soften our pride when it stands between us and reconciliation and grant us courage to forgive those who have wronged us.

May our acts of mercy mirror Your own, drawing others into the freedom of Your love.

Empower us to heal broken relationships with words of kindness and deeds of service.

In releasing our hurts, remind us that we, too, are released—captives made free by Your redeeming love. In Jesus' name we pray, Amen.

8
Faith and Fear

Overcoming Life's Anxieties with Trust

"Do not be anxious about anything, but in every situation, by prayer and petition, with thanksgiving, present your requests to God. And the peace of God, which transcends all understanding, will guard your hearts and your minds in Christ Jesus." — **Philippians 4:6-7**

In the intricate tapestry of human experience, faith and fear often intermingle, shaping our perceptions and guiding our responses to the challenges we face. While fear is a primal emotion stemming from our instinct for survival, faith acts as a counterbalance, providing comfort and hope amid life's uncertainties.

In this essay, we will explore how trust—whether in ourselves, others, or a higher power—serves as a vital resource for transcending anxiety and navigating the tumultuous waters of life's anxieties.

Fear, by its very nature, can be paralyzing. It manifests in various forms—fear of the unknown, fear of failure, fear of rejection, and an overarching existential fear that can sometimes feel insurmountable. These fears can lead to anxiety, a state that drains our mental energy and colors our worldview with shades of pessimism.

For many, anxiety becomes a constant companion, hindering personal growth and stifling the pursuit of happiness. However, within this shadow lies the potent light of faith, a belief system that can counteract the grip of fear.

Faith, often perceived in a religious context, extends beyond spiritual beliefs. It can encompass trust in one's abilities, confidence in supportive relationships, and assurance in the unfolding of life's processes. When we cultivate faith, we create a psychological buffer against anxiety. This trust allows us to confront our fears head-on, rather than allowing them to dictate our lives.

For instance, individuals facing career uncertainties may experience a paralyzing fear of failure. By fostering faith in their skills and maintaining a belief that opportunities will arise, they can take actionable steps towards their goals, transforming anxiety into motivation.

Moreover, trust in interpersonal relationships can significantly mitigate feelings of anxiety. When individuals form deep connections with others, their sense of security increases. Knowing there are people who care and believe in us creates a safety net that alleviates some of life's pressures.

Supportive relationships encourage open communication and sharing of fears, which can be cathartic and empowering. For example, a person grappling with anxiety may find solace in discussing their fears with a friend or therapist, allowing them to gain perspective and, in turn, foster a renewed sense of faith in their journey.

On a broader scale, many people find solace in faith through spirituality or religion. This path offers not only a sense of community but also the reassurance of a higher purpose. The teachings of various faiths frequently emphasize the importance of trusting in a plan greater than oneself, which can alleviate the burden of anxiety.

For instance, many religious traditions advocate the notion that surrendering to faith can lead to inner peace. By embracing these teachings, individuals can find strength in vulnerability, allowing them to confront life's challenges with renewed courage.

However, faith does not eliminate fear. Instead, it provides a framework for understanding and navigating it. The act of trusting—whether in oneself, others, or a higher power—does not mean the absence of fear; rather, it signifies a decision to move forward despite it.

Acknowledging fears candidly while simultaneously placing faith in the journey's potential can empower individuals to cultivate resilience. This resilience is crucial in overcoming the inevitable trials of life and can transform anxiety into a catalyst for personal growth.

In conclusion, the interplay between faith and fear is a profound aspect of the human condition. While fear can bind us in chains, faith can liberate us from the anxieties that seek to control our lives.

By nurturing trust in ourselves, our relationships, and the universe's serendipities, we can forge a path through life's uncertainties. In doing so, we learn that faith is not a denial of fear but a powerful tool to overcome it, allowing us to embrace life's adventures with courage and conviction. Through this journey of trust, we can transform anxiety into a steppingstone toward a more fulfilled and authentic existence.

Faith Outshines Fear

Charles E. Cravey

When shadows stir within the restless mind,
And troubled thoughts like phantoms fill the heart,
Faith serves as lamp when path is hard to find,
Its gentle flame dispels the gloomier part.

Though fear may whisper doubts of coming day,
And anxious mists obscure the way ahead,
We trust the One who guides through storm and sway,
Whose word secures our steps where we are led.

In every breath of prayer, our spirits rise,
A quiet strength that stills the churning sea.
With trust we hang our hope beyond the skies,
And claim the peace from Christ's own victory.

So, when the coward shadows call our name,
We'll stand in faith, unbroken by their claim.

Closing Prayer: A Prayer to Cast Out Fear

Heavenly Father, Giver of Perfect Peace, we lift our anxious hearts to You and lay aside the worries that entangle our days. Teach us to trust in Your steadfast care, knowing that Your love outlasts every fleeting fear. In moments of trembling doubt, draw us close and remind us that You hold us fast, guiding our steps through calm and storm alike.

Help us to exchange our fears for faith, to surrender each burden at Your throne through prayer. May Your peace, which surpasses all understanding, guard our hearts and minds in Christ Jesus, anchoring us in hope. In Jesus' name we pray, Amen.

9
The Blessing of Trials

Growing Stronger Through Adversity

"Consider it pure joy, my brothers and sisters, whenever you face trials of many kinds, because you know that the testing of your faith produces perseverance." — James 1:2-3

Adversity is an inevitable component of the human experience. It presents itself in various forms, whether as financial hardship, personal loss, health challenges, or societal issues. While trials can be painful and disheartening, they often emerge as profound teachers, imparting valuable lessons and fostering resilience.

The concept that trials can be blessings may seem counterintuitive, yet through facing difficulties, individuals cultivate strength, develop empathy, and enhance their problem-solving capabilities.

Primarily, trials often serve as catalysts for personal growth. They compel individuals to confront their limitations and expand their capacities. For instance, consider the story of Thomas Edison, who famously failed thousands of times before inventing the light bulb. Each setback provided Edison with insights and wisdom that drove him toward success. These experiences not only refine skills but also build a sense of perseverance. This steadfastness is essential as it transforms failures into steppingstones, allowing individuals to navigate future challenges with greater confidence.

Moreover, adversity nurtures empathy and compassion. Experiencing hardship often leads to a deeper understanding of others' struggles. When individuals face their own trials, they become more attuned to the pain and challenges of those around them.

For example, a person who has battled illness may become a source of support for others facing similar circumstances, offering not just emotional understanding but also practical advice. This sense of shared experience fosters community and belonging, advocating for kindness and support in a world that can often feel isolating.

Furthermore, overcoming difficulties can enhance problem-solving skills. When faced with unexpected challenges, individuals are often pushed to think creatively and develop innovative solutions. This adaptability is a crucial life skill.

For instance, businesses that confront economic downturns are frequently forced to reassess their strategies and pivot to survive. In this way, adversity does not merely present obstacles but compels us to innovate and adapt, leading to greater success and efficiency in both personal and professional realms.

The psychological benefits of overcoming adversity are equally significant. Studies illustrate that individuals who have navigated trials often report higher levels of gratitude and appreciation for life.

Facing challenges facilitates a perspective shift; the small inconveniences of daily life become less daunting when viewed against the backdrop of significant struggles. This renewed outlook fosters resilience and a greater appreciation for the positive aspects of life, nurturing mental and emotional well-being in the process.

In summary, the notion that trials can serve as blessings is rooted in the profound transformations that arise from facing adversity. Through challenges, individuals discover their inner strength, cultivate empathy toward others, and enhance their problem-solving abilities.

These experiences are not merely obstacles but rather steppingstones on the journey toward personal growth and fulfillment. As we navigate the trials of life, it is essential to embrace them as opportunities for development, recognizing that our struggles enrich us, preparing us to face whatever lies ahead with resilience and grace.

The Blessing of Trials

Charles E. Cravey

When storms descend and shadows cloak the day,
And thunder's roar assails the fragile heart,
Yet in the furnace flame our faith holds sway,
Unveiling strength concealed in every part.

Through tears and trials, grit forms unshakable,
Each pang of pain matures the tender seed.
Adversity refines the soul, unbreakable,
And shapes our purpose for the path we need.

No hardship falls without a higher aim,
Nor sorrow comes apart from sovereign grace.
What feels like loss heralds a faith aflame,
Till every wound reveals a holy trace.

So, bless the test that teaches how to rise—
In every trial, God's own blessing lies.

Closing Prayer: A Prayer for Perseverance

Heavenly Father,

You are our Rock when trials press upon us and our Comfort in every season of sorrow. We thank You for the refining work You accomplish through adversity. Grant us eyes to see Your hand at work in every challenge and hearts that trust You even when the way is hard.

Strengthen our resolve, deepen our faith, and shape our character so that we emerge more like Christ in endurance and hope. Help us to encourage one another with stories of Your faithfulness, that together we might stand unwavering, anchored in Your love. In Jesus' name we pray, Amen.

10
Sharing Your light

The Joy of Serving Others

"In the same way, let your light shine before others, that they may see your good deeds and glorify your Father in heaven." — **Matthew 5:16**

In a world that often seems consumed by self-interest and individual pursuits, the idea of serving others stands out as a beacon of hope and community. "Sharing your light" is more than a metaphor; it is a call to action that encourages individuals to use their gifts, talents, and time to make a positive impact on the lives of others.

The joy derived from serving others not only transforms the recipient but also enriches the giver, creating a cycle of kindness and compassion that can illuminate even the darkest corners of our communities.

At the heart of service is the concept of empathy. When we choose to share our light, we step into the shoes of others, seeking to understand their struggles, dreams, and aspirations. This empathetic approach fosters connections that transcend superficial interactions, promoting a sense of unity and belonging.

For instance, volunteering at a local shelter not only meets the immediate needs of those facing hardship but also nurtures a sense of community among volunteers and beneficiaries alike. The shared experiences create lasting bonds, as individuals learn from one another, celebrating not just differences, but also shared humanity.

Moreover, serving others instills a sense of purpose. In today's fast-paced society, it is easy to become lost in the pursuit of personal success and material wealth. Yet, many find that true fulfillment comes not from what we accumulate but from what we contribute.

Whether mentoring a young student, participating in environmental cleanups, or providing emotional support to a friend in need, acts of service remind us of our interconnectedness and the ripple effect of our actions. Each small gesture of kindness can lead to meaningful change, inspiring others to pay it forward, thereby creating a chain reaction of goodwill.

The joy of serving others is also reflected in the personal growth that often accompanies altruistic behaviors. Engaging in community service encourages the development of valuable life skills such as communication, leadership, and problem-solving. As we face new challenges while serving, we also become more resilient and adaptable.

The discomfort of stepping outside our comfort zones opens the door to understanding diverse perspectives and fosters personal growth. This transformation not only changes us for the better but also empowers us to be more effective agents of change within our communities.

Moreover, science supports the notion that altruistic behaviors contribute positively to our well-being. Studies have shown that acts of kindness release endorphins, creating what is known as a "helper's high." This natural high not only boosts our mood but also promotes mental and emotional health, reducing stress and anxiety. In this way, serving others becomes a form of self-care.

By contributing our time and energy to uplift others, we also nourish our own spirits, leading to a more fulfilling and enriched life.

Importantly, the joy of serving others is not limited to grand gestures but can be found in the simplest of actions. A smile shared with a stranger, a meal prepared for a neighbor, or a listening ear offered in times of distress can equally spread light in the world.

Each act of kindness, no matter how small, holds the power to illuminate someone's day. By cultivating an attitude of service in our daily lives, we learn to recognize opportunities to share our light in both ordinary and extraordinary moments.

In conclusion, "Sharing Your Light: The Joy of Serving Others" encapsulates the transformative power of altruism. The interconnectedness of our lives emphasizes the significance of empathy, community, and personal growth achieved through acts of service.

As we intentionally seek to brighten the lives of those around us, we not only enhance the world but also ignite a sense of joy within ourselves. Let us embrace the call to share our light, creating a brighter, more compassionate future for all. In doing so, we discover that the true essence of life lies not in what we have, but in how we choose to illuminate the lives of others.

The Hand That Lights the Way

Charles E. Cravey

When weary souls are lost in self-bound gloom,
The faintest spark of kindness stirs the flame.
A tender hand can chase away the doom,
And point the way toward hope in Jesus' name.

Through acts of service, lives are mirrored bright,
As lamps we bear, dispelling sin's deep shade.
In giving love, we walk in holy light,
The path of grace by selfless hearts is laid.

The bread we break, the words we kindly share,
Become the very gift we did not know.
Our gifts reflect the One who bids us care.
In every smile His boundless mercy shows.

So let us shine, with arms of love outspread,
And share the light our risen Lord has shed.

Closing Prayer: A Prayer to Share His Light

Heavenly Father of Compassionate Love,

Thank You for entrusting us with the blessing of service, that in giving we receive, and in lifting others we are lifted. Teach us to see every need as an opportunity to share Your grace and every heart as a canvas for Your kindness.

May our hands be steady, our voices soft, and our spirits eager to serve. Let our deeds—no matter how small—be beacons that guide others toward Your heart. Shape us into vessels of Your light, that all who encounter us might glimpse Your goodness and give You praise. In Jesus' name we pray, Amen.

11
Biblical Joy

Lessons from Scripture on Happiness

"You make known to me the path of life; in your presence there is fullness of joy; at your right hand are pleasures forevermore." — **Psalm 16:11**

Joy is a profound and often elusive emotion, sought after by individuals across cultures and eras. In a world increasingly obsessed with fleeting pleasures and transient happiness, the Bible offers enduring wisdom on the nature of joy, its significance, and the pathways to attaining it.

This essay explores the concept of biblical joy, drawing on scripture to illuminate how true happiness can be found through faith, community, gratitude, and purpose.

The Foundation of Joy in Faith

At the heart of biblical joy is the relationship between individuals and God. Scriptures like Psalm 16:11 articulate this profound truth, stating, "You make known to me the path of life; in your presence there is fullness of joy; at your right hand are pleasures forevermore." This verse suggests that true joy originates from being in communion with God, implying that spiritual fulfillment surpasses external circumstances.

Furthermore, in the New Testament, the Apostle Paul writes in Philippians 4:4, "Rejoice in the Lord always; again I will say, rejoice." This command to rejoice is rooted not in changing situations but in a steadfast relationship with God.

The biblical concept of joy is closely intertwined with faith—it's an inner quality that persists even amidst trials, as emphasized in James 1:2-3: "Count it all joy, my brothers, when you meet trials of various kinds." Here, joy is not the absence of difficulties but the assurance that God's presence and purpose remain constant.

Joy in Community and Fellowship

Another pivotal lesson from scripture on happiness is the importance of community. The Bible emphasizes that joy is best experienced in relationships—with God and others. In the Book of Acts, we see the early church embodying this principle as they shared their lives, possessions, and faith with one another.

Acts 2:46-47 states, "And day by day, attending the temple together and breaking bread in their homes, they received their food with glad and generous hearts, praising God and having favor with all the people." The joy of the early Christians was rooted in their communal experience, not just individual spirituality.

Moreover, both the Old and New Testaments highlight the significance of building each other up. In Romans 12:15, Paul instructs believers to "Rejoice with those who rejoice, weep with those who weep." This empathetic sharing of experiences fosters connections and cultivates an environment where joy can flourish. The collective joy of a community enriches individual happiness, illustrating that true joy is accentuated in fellowship.

The Role of Gratitude

Gratitude is another critical aspect of biblical joy. The act of recognizing and appreciating God's blessings creates an atmosphere conducive to happiness. In 1 Thessalonians 5:16-18, Paul advises, "Rejoice always, pray without ceasing, give thanks in all circumstances; for this is the will of God in Christ Jesus for you." This directive highlights a vital connection between thankfulness and joy.

By focusing on gratitude, individuals shift their perspective from what they lack to what they possess, fostering a sense of contentment regardless of circumstances. Psalms 100:4 invites believers to "Enter his gates with thanksgiving, and his courts with praise!" This attitude of gratitude is transformative, enabling individuals to experience joy even in the mundane aspects of life.

Purpose and Service

Finally, scripture underscores that joy arises from purposeful living and serving others. In Proverbs 17:22, it is stated, "A joyful heart is good medicine, but a crushed spirit dries up the bones." This verse conveys that joy is not merely a personal pursuit but a force that revitalizes individuals and communities.

Jesus exemplified this principle of joy through service, teaching that true happiness comes from giving rather than receiving. In Acts 20:35, it is stated, "It is more blessed to give than to receive."

Serving others creates a ripple effect of joy, enriching the one who serves and those being served. In this light, the pursuit of happiness becomes intertwined with the act of selflessness and community engagement.

Conclusion

Biblical joy presents a transformative perspective on happiness, inviting individuals to seek fulfillment beyond worldly pursuits. By anchoring joy in faith, fostering community, practicing gratitude, and embracing purposeful service, believers can cultivate a resilient and abiding happiness.

The lessons from scripture remind us that joy is not merely an emotion but a condition of the heart, deeply rooted in our relationship with God and others. In a world searching for lasting happiness, the Bible provides a clear path to discovering true joy, illuminating the way to a life rich in purpose and meaningful connections.

Wellspring of Joy

Charles E. Cravey

When morning breaks with laughter in its gleam,
And waking hearts behold the sky's embrace,
We taste the depth of Christ's unending stream.
A joy that time nor sorrow can erase.

In every trial we learn to sing again.
As faith rewrites the melody of strife,
When tears fall soft like gentle summer rain,
They water seeds of peace that shape our life.

No fleeting spark, but constant radiant light,
The joy divine sustains our pilgrim way.
Through every shadow, through the darkest night,
It guides our souls to dance in endless day.

A treasure found in Him who sets us free—
In Christ, our joy abides eternally.

Closing Prayer: A Prayer to Abide in Joy

Heavenly Father of Joyful Presence,
We praise You for the wellspring of joy You pour into our hearts. Teach us to rejoice in Your love, that our rejoicing springs not from circumstances but from Your unchanging grace. Amid life's highs and lows, may Your joy be our refuge and strength. Grant us eyes to see Your blessings, voices to proclaim Your goodness, and hearts to share Your joy with all we meet. In every moment, may we abide in the fullness of Your delight. In Jesus' name we pray, Amen.

12
Trusting God's Timing

Patience in a Fast-Paced World

"To everything there is a season, and a time for every matter under heaven." — **Ecclesiastes 3:1**

In an age defined by instant gratification, the concept of patience often feels foreign. From fast food to one-click deliveries, the modern world trains us to expect immediate results. Yet, amidst the whirlwind of our daily lives, one profound truth remains:

trusting in God's timing is essential for fostering deeper faith, personal growth, and lasting joy.

In this essay, we will explore the importance of patience, the challenges it presents, and how it can be cultivated through a greater reliance on divine timing.

At the heart of trusting God's timing is the understanding that life unfolds according to a divine plan, one that may not always align with our own expectations or desires. Scripture emphasizes this principle, reminding us in Ecclesiastes 3:1 that "to everything, there is a season, and a time for every matter under heaven." This verse encapsulates the essence of faith: recognizing that God's timing is perfect, even when it diverges from our personal timeline.

One of the most significant challenges we face in a fast-paced world is the tendency to equate busyness with productivity. Society often glorifies those who consistently hustle, leaving little room for rest or reflection. This mindset tends to breed anxiety and discontent, as we constantly compare our lives to others, questioning why we have not yet achieved our goals.

By choosing to trust in God's timing, however, we can shift this perspective and embrace a more profound sense of peace. We are reminded that not every season of life requires relentless activity; there are moments intended for preparation, healing, and growth.

Moreover, trusting in God's timing invites us to develop resilience in the face of adversity. When challenges arise—be it in our relationships, careers, or personal endeavors—our initial response may be impatience and frustration. Yet, these periods of waiting often serve a purpose far greater than we can comprehend.

In Romans 5:3-4, Paul writes, "Not only that, but we rejoice in our sufferings, knowing that suffering produces endurance, and endurance produces character, and character produces hope." Through periods of waiting and uncertainty, we cultivate traits such as perseverance and trust that deepen our character and prepare us for future blessings.

In practical terms, developing patience in our spiritual journey requires intentional practice. This practice can manifest in many ways, from dedicating time for prayer and reflection to seeking guidance from Scripture. Engaging in communal worship also plays a crucial role; being surrounded by a faith community fosters accountability and encouragement.

It is through these shared experiences that we learn from one another's journeys, gaining insight into how to navigate the complexities of life while waiting for God's timing.

Another essential aspect of trusting God's timing is the recognition that it often leads to greater blessings than what we initially envisioned. When we relinquish control, we open ourselves to possibilities beyond our comprehension.

There are countless stories in the Bible that illustrate this truth—Joseph's journey from slavery to royalty, Esther's rise to become a queen for such a time as this, and even Jesus' delayed arrival to heal Lazarus all serve to remind us that God's plans are infinitely wiser than our own. In surrendering our timelines, we allow God to work in us and through us, often providing outcomes richer than we dared to hope for.

In conclusion, trusting God's timing is an antidote to the impatience that permeates our fast-paced world. By embracing patience as a spiritual practice, we learn to align ourselves with divine purpose, developing endurance and character along the way.

As we journey through life, let us remember to pause, reflect, and trust in the beautiful intricacies of God's timing. In doing so, we not only cultivate peace within ourselves but also invite the blessings of a life lived in harmony with God's divine plan. Thus, in a society driven by urgency, we discover the transformative power of patience—one that leads us to a deeper and more meaningful existence.

The Perfect Hour

Charles E. Cravey

When days seem long and patience wears us thin,
We learn to wait upon the Lord's sure hand.
Though hidden roads lie veiled in night's dark din,
His guiding light unfolds His sovereign plan.

Each moment held beneath His watchful eye
Becomes a seed of grace in fertile soil.
Through seasons slow or swifter than a sigh,
He forms our hearts without our strain or toil.

No hurried step can hasten what He ordains.
Nor anxious breath unbind His quiet grace.
In stillness we receive what hope sustains,
And trust the pace of His appointed place.

So let us rest where faith and waiting meet,
For in His time, His promises are sweet.

Closing Prayer: Trusting in His Timing

Heavenly Father of Endless Wisdom,
You know our every need before we speak a word, and Your timing is perfect beyond our understanding. Teach us to rest in Your sovereignty when our plans delay or diverge. Grant us the grace to trust Your timetable—believing that each pause prepares us for what lies ahead, and every delay reveals Your deeper purpose.

Help us embrace the waiting seasons with hope, steadfast in faith and rich in patience. May we find peace in Your presence, confident that in Your perfect hour, all things align for our good and Your glory.

In Jesus' name we pray, Amen.

13
Worship in Everyday Life

Finding God in the Mundane

"Therefore, I urge you, brothers and sisters, in view of God's mercy, to offer your bodies as a living sacrifice, holy and pleasing to God—this is your true and proper worship." — **Romans 12:1**

In the fast-paced world we inhabit, days often collapse into a blur of responsibilities, obligations, and routines. The divine can seem distant, overshadowed by the incessant demands of daily life. Yet, within the chaos and monotony, there lies a profound opportunity for worship—an invitation to seek and find God in the mundane moments that compose our existence.

This essay explores the concept of worship beyond the walls of traditional religious settings, emphasizing the significance of recognizing the sacred in everyday activities, interactions, and experiences.

Historically, worship has been defined by formal rituals, liturgy, and organized gatherings within houses of worship. While these practices serve a vital role in communal faith, they can inadvertently lead to the misconception that worship is confined to specific times and places.

In contrast, the essence of genuine worship transcends such boundaries. It can flourish in the quiet moments of the day—whether it's savoring a warm cup of coffee in the morning, listening to a friend's troubles with compassion, or even tending to the garden. Each action can be infused with reverence and gratitude, transforming the ordinary into extraordinary expressions of faith.

One profound way to reframe our understanding of worship is through the lens of mindfulness. Mindfulness invites us to engage fully with our present experiences, encouraging a profound awareness of the simplicity surrounding us. In practicing mindfulness, we are able to witness the beauty and complexity of life in all its forms.

A walk in nature, for example, can become an act of worship when we consciously appreciate the vibrant colors of the flowers, the gentle rustling of the leaves, or the chirping of the birds. In such moments, we recognize the divine presence in creation, awakening a sense of awe and gratitude that permeates our hearts.

Additionally, meaningful interactions with others offer a canvas for worship. Acts of kindness, patience, and love towards family, friends, and even strangers can form a sacred connection that aligns with the teachings of many faith traditions.

When we approach our daily encounters as opportunities to express love and compassion, we participate in a form of worship that honors the inherent dignity of every person. The act of listening attentively to someone's story or offering support in times of need can serve as tangible manifestations of our faith, woven seamlessly into the fabric of our everyday lives.

Furthermore, daily chores and responsibilities present unique opportunities for worship that are often overlooked. Whether it is cooking a meal, cleaning our living spaces, or completing tasks at work, these activities can be transformed into acts of devotion.

By approaching them with an attitude of gratitude and intention, we can find joy in serving those we love and fulfilling our obligations. Each task, infused with purpose and conscientiousness, becomes an expression of our commitment to the values we hold sacred, promoting a sense of peace and fulfillment.

Incorporating rituals into our everyday routines can also enhance our capacity for worship in the mundane. Simple practices—such as pausing for a moment of gratitude before a meal, setting aside time for reflection at the end of the day, or creating a peaceful space for prayer—can serve as reminders of the divine presence surrounding us. Such rituals anchor us in our intentionality and shift our focus to the myriad blessings that each day holds.

The journey of finding God in the mundane involves a radical shift in perspective. It requires us to cultivate an awareness that the sacred exists not just in the extraordinary; it permeates every corner of our lives. By choosing to embrace the everyday moments as opportunities for worship, we can deepen our spiritual connection and foster a sense of belonging to something greater than ourselves.

In conclusion, worship in everyday life invites us to seek and celebrate the divine woven into the fabric of our daily experiences. Through mindfulness, meaningful connections, intentional actions, and simple rituals, we unlock the potential for recognizing God in the ordinary.

By cultivating this awareness, we can transform our mundane routines into sacred practices, enriching both our spiritual lives and the world around us. As we navigate the complexities of life, let us remember that every moment holds the potential for worship; we need only to open our hearts and minds to the divine present within our everyday existence.

Worship in Simple Things

Charles E. Cravey

When dawn begins, we lift an unspoken song.
In every breath, a hymn to grace untold.
Each humble task we fold into His song,
As worship blooms in mornings bright and bold.

The kettle's whistle rises, a sacred sign,
A steaming cup delivers gentle care.
In simple rites, we witness love divine,
Revealing worship found in simple fare.

The gentle sweep of broom on wood and stone,
A quiet dance of faith in every chore.

Each dish we wash becomes a prayer well known,
As we serve Christ in tasks we can't ignore.

So may our deeds resound to bless Your name,
And every joy and care be praised the same.

Closing Prayer: A Prayer for Sacred Moments

Heavenly Father, in the bounty of each new day, teach us to recognize every moment as an opportunity for worship. May our mornings, meals, and mundane tasks be offered as living sacrifices, holy and pleasing to You. Open our eyes to the sacred woven through daily routines, that in each simple chore we might encounter Your presence anew. Grant us grateful hearts to embrace the gift of presence and to serve You with joy in all we do. In Jesus' name we pray, Amen.

14
Living in Hope

Looking Forward to Eternity

"Praise be to the God and Father of our Lord Jesus Christ! In his great mercy he has given us new birth into a living hope through the resurrection of Jesus Christ from the dead." — **1 Peter 1:3**

In a world often shadowed by uncertainty and impermanence, the concept of hope emerges as a guiding light, particularly in the context of eternity. Every person, regardless of their beliefs or background, grapples with questions about their existence, purpose, and what lies beyond.

Living in hope, therefore, becomes profoundly significant—not merely as a fantasy of life beyond death but as a transformative force that shapes our present and future.

At its core, hope is intrinsically linked to the human condition. It fuels our dreams, inspires resilience, and pushes us toward achieving our aspirations. However, when viewed through the prism of eternity, hope transcends individual desires and points toward a deeper understanding of our existence. It invites us to contemplate life's ultimate purpose and the legacy we wish to leave behind.

The contemplation of eternity can serve as a driving force for many people, motivating them to live meaningful lives in the present while looking forward to a future that extends far beyond their current reality.

Throughout history, various cultures and religions have depicted eternity in diverse ways, often imbuing their narratives with ethical frameworks that guide moral behavior. Christianity, for instance, speaks of eternal life through faith and redemption, framing hope within the context of divine promise.

Similarly, in Eastern philosophies, the cycle of life, death, and rebirth is seen as a continuous journey toward enlightenment. Regardless of the tradition, the promise of eternity instills a sense of purpose and a responsibility to live a life grounded in love, compassion, and service to others.

Living with the hope of eternity encourages individuals to engage with life more fully. This perspective prompts a reevaluation of how we spend our time and how we cultivate our relationships. If we perceive our existence as a fleeting moment in a much grander narrative, we may find greater value in the connections we forge and the kindness we extend.

In this way, hope can serve as a catalyst for positive action, prompting individuals to contribute toward the collective good and strive for a legacy that reflects their values and beliefs.

Moreover, the anticipation of eternity provides solace in times of distress and loss. The inevitability of life's trials often weighs heavy on the human spirit. However, hope—a belief in something greater than ourselves—can empower individuals to endure suffering and face adversities with courage. It offers comfort in grief, as the hope for reunion or transcendence can fortify the heart against despair.

In the face of mortality, hope emerges as a form of resilience that enables us to navigate through life's uncertainties with faith and strength.

Yet, hope must also be coupled with action. Living in hope of eternity does not imply a passive awaiting of afterlife rewards. Instead, it calls for intentionality in our daily actions and choices. A life lived in hope serves as a commitment to bettering ourselves and the world around us.

This journey is not merely about personal fulfillment but about contributing to a collective future. By embodying the values we associate with eternity—love, justice, peace, and understanding—we can create a world that mirrors the ideals we aspire to in our vision of eternity.

As we reflect on the idea of living in hope while looking forward to eternity, it becomes clear that this mindset is paramount to fostering a fulfilling, purposeful life. In recognizing our shared human experience, we cultivate empathy toward others and acknowledge our interconnectedness. Life, with its myriad challenges and uncertainties, invites us to choose hope as a response—a choice that has the power to illuminate our path and influence those around us.

In conclusion, living in hope while looking forward to eternity challenges us to embrace life with open hearts and minds. It inspires us to reflect on our values, fostering a deeper understanding of what it means to be human.

As we carry our hopes forward, let us remember that each moment counts, and every action can contribute to a legacy of love, compassion, and unity that reaches far beyond our earthly existence. Hope does not merely prepare us for eternity; it empowers us to actively create a brighter world today.

Dawn of Eternal Hope

Charles E. Cravey

When earthly shadows press upon the soul,
And fleeting joys seem lost to passing years,
Yet hope springs forth from wells that never roll,
Unfading light that calms our deepest fears.

Though tempests rage and dreams seem cast away,
We lift our gaze beyond the veiling night.
For Christ has broken dawn of endless day,
Dispelling doubt with sacred morning light.

This living hope, a seed that faith has sown,
Blooms in the heart, unbound by time or space.

> Its gentle roots through every storm have grown,
> Sustaining spirits with redeeming grace.
>
> So let us walk where promises unfold,
> Our hope secured in love that never grows old.

Closing Prayer: A Prayer to Abide in Eternal Hope

Heavenly Father of Living Hope, we thank You for the promise that reaches beyond our circumstances and anchors our souls in Christ. When doubts assail and trials press upon our hearts, remind us of the resurrection dawn that casts out every shadow.

Teach us to live each day in the strength of Your unending love. Let our lives reflect the steadfast light of hope, offering comfort and courage to those who feel weary and afraid. May we bear this hope like a lamp, guiding others toward the promise of eternity.

In Jesus' name we pray, Amen.

15
Spreading Sunshine

How Acts of Kindness Transform Us

"A generous person will prosper; whoever refreshes others will be refreshed." — **Proverbs 11:25**

In a world that often seems engulfed in chaos and disillusionment, the simple act of kindness stands out as a beacon of hope and positivity. "Spreading Sunshine" is not merely a charming metaphor; it embodies a transformative force capable of altering the fabric of our daily lives and relationships. From small gestures to significant acts, kindness has the power to uplift our spirits, foster community, and even catalyze lasting change.

This essay explores how each act of kindness—both given and received—shapes our identity, nurtures our emotional well-being, and creates a more compassionate world.

The Ripple Effect of Kindness

One of the most profound aspects of kindness is its infectious nature. When a person receives a kind gesture, they are often inspired to pay it forward. This "ripple effect" can lead to a chain reaction of positive interactions that spreads far beyond an individual act.

Scientific studies suggest that witnessing acts of kindness can evoke feelings of happiness and an increased propensity to help others. For instance, a simple smile or a helping hand can inspire someone to perform a similar act, creating a network of goodwill that strengthens community bonds.

As kindness is shared, it enriches the fabric of society, reminding us that humanity can unite through even the smallest of gestures.

Kindness as a Path to Personal Growth

Acts of kindness not only benefit those we help but also foster our own personal growth and fulfillment. Engaging in altruistic behavior can enhance our sense of purpose and belonging, contributing to improved mental health. Studies indicate that individuals who regularly practice kindness report lower levels of stress and anxiety, improved mood, and greater life satisfaction.

The neurological mechanisms behind this transformation are fascinating; acts of kindness stimulate the release of oxytocin, a hormone associated with bonding, which encourages a feeling of warmth and connection. Thus, being kind can be a powerful antidote to the isolation and negativity that frequently permeate modern life.

Courageous Kindness: Overcoming Barriers

While performing acts of kindness may seem straightforward, they can sometimes require a great deal of courage and vulnerability. In today's fast-paced society, taking the time to help others can feel daunting, especially when faced with prejudices or societal judgment.

However, overcoming these barriers allows for a deeper understanding and connection with others. Acts of kindness directed toward those who are different from us—be it through racial, cultural, or socioeconomic lines—foster empathy and dismantle stereotypes. Engaging with individuals outside our comfort zones not only broadens our perspectives but also promotes inclusivity, making our communities stronger and more cohesive.

Creating a Culture of Kindness

To harness the transformative power of kindness, we must actively cultivate a culture of kindness in our homes, workplaces, and communities. This begins with education and awareness, teaching individuals about the importance of empathy and compassion from an early age.

Schools and organizations can integrate programs that encourage kindness, such as volunteering initiatives or mentorship programs, which not only allow individuals to give back but also strengthen their self-image and develop leadership skills. Furthermore, social media can be a powerful tool for spreading kindness; campaigns that promote positivity and gratitude can reach a vast audience, encouraging a global commitment to promoting acts of kindness.

Conclusion

In conclusion, "spreading sunshine" through acts of kindness has the potential to transform not only the individuals who receive kindness but also those who give it. By recognizing the ripple effects of our actions, embracing opportunities for personal growth, overcoming barriers to kindness, and creating a culture that values compassion, we can foster a kinder, more connected world. Each small gesture of kindness contributes to a larger movement toward positivity, proving that even in the darkest times, we have the power to illuminate the lives of others—and ourselves—through simple acts of love and generosity.

Let us all strive to spread sunshine in our everyday lives, illuminating the path to a brighter, more compassionate future.

Spreading Sunshine

Charles E. Cravey

When gloom descends and hearts are pressed with care,
A single spark of kindness lights the day.
Soft words and humble deeds reveal we share
A ray of hope that drives the dark away.

In giving, grace unfolds its subtle art,
To lift each weary soul from depths of pain.
Like dewdrops glistening on a fragile heart,
These gifts of love remind us we remain.

No act too small to warm the coldest soul,
No word too soft to stir the faintest voice.
In kindness Christ revives what sin stole,
And bids our hearts in hope and love rejoice.

So may our steps be light and spirits free,
That every place we tread may brighter be.

Closing Prayer: A Prayer to Spread Kindness

Heavenly Father of Endless Compassion,
Thank You for the gift of kindness, a simple blessing that scatters warmth and hope where it is needed most. Teach us to recognize every moment as an opportunity to shine Your light through our words and deeds.

Empower us to serve with open hands and compassionate hearts, reflecting the generous love You've lavished on us. May our small acts become beacons of Your grace, encouraging weary souls and drawing others into Your embrace.

Grant that in giving, we ourselves may be refreshed and renewed, living testimonies to the transforming power of Christ's love. Let our lives overflow with generosity, that we might spread Your sunshine across every path we wander.

In Jesus' name we pray, Amen.

Afterword

It has been my deep joy to walk alongside you through these pages, exploring how light breaks through darkness, gratitude awakens our souls, and grace transforms our hearts. Each chapter has offered a sonnet to stir your spirit, a prayer to steady your steps, and a Scripture to anchor your hope. Together, they form a tapestry of front-porch faith—inviting you to live in open welcome, generous hospitality, and unwavering trust.

As life unfolds beyond this book, return to these reflections whenever you need renewal. Read the sonnets aloud on a quiet morning, lean into the prayers when dusk settles heavy on your shoulders, and let the Scriptures linger in your mind as you serve and love your neighbors. These words were crafted to become rhythms in your daily walk—a companion for every season of your faith journey.

May this book settle into your heart like a bench on a shady porch—a place to rest, to wrestle, to rejoice. Let it remind you that faith is not a one-time choice but a series of small, holy moments: a smile to a stranger, a whispered "thank You" in the chaos, a hand offered in forgiveness, a lamp carried into someone else's night.

Now, as you step forward, may the God of morning light and evening calm go before you. May your days be bright with purpose, your nights rich with peace, and your front porch ever ready to receive both friend and stranger. In the shelter of His love, may you find strength to share that love unreservedly—spreading sunshine wherever you wander.

The Rev. Dr. Charles E. Cravey

www.ingramcontent.com/pod-product-compliance
Lightning Source LLC
LaVergne TN
LVHW011209080426
835508LV00007B/689